Jennie Lee's Homework Project

n be made

~fe.co

in

About the Playwright

WILLIAM HERSHAW: Poet, musician and songwriter.

Hershaw has written poetry in both Scots and English; his pamphlet *Winter Song* won the Callum MacDonald Memorial Award in 2003, and he won the McCash Prize for Scots Poetry in 2011. In 2007 he collaborated with sculptor David Annand, writing the poem 'God The Miner' which is inscribed on the statue *The Prop* as part of the Lochgelly Regeneration Project. He was funded by Fife Council to write musical settings for the poems of the legendary Fife poet and playwright Joe Corrie: in November 2012 *Cage Load Of Men: The Joe Corrie Project* by The Bowhill Players was released. He has co-edited the literary magazine *Fras*.

Grace Note published three of his Scots language plays in 2016, including a translation of Shakespeare's *Tempest*, and a novel, *Tammy Norrie*. His play with Ann McCluskey, *An Iolaire* was premiered in March 2016 at the Netherbow Arts Theatre, performed by pupils from Tynecastle High School and Stenhouse Primary.

Jennie Lee's Homework Project

A play by William Hershaw

Jenny Lee's Homework Project
First published 2017 by Grace Note Publications C.I.C.
Grange of Locherlour, Ochtertyre, PH7 4JS, Scotland

books@gracenotereading.co.uk
www.gracenotepublications.co.uk

ISBN 978-1-907676-88-8

First Performance of *Jennie Lee's Homework Project* by the Benarty Primary School
at 67-69 Lochleven Road, Lochore, Fife, Scotland

A CIP catalogue record fo[...] [...]ibrary

CONTENTS

Introduction

Fifty years ago, a visitor to the coal-blackened post industrial landscape at Lochore Meadows would have been surprised to find a twelfth century castle half-buried among the spillage of bings, slag heaps, twisted metal and derelict pithead buildings. That same visitor might have been even more surprised to learn that long before that stone built castle was erected, Iron Age folk had lived on a crannog on an island on the same spot. It seems that folk have lived here, below Benarty Hill, for a very long time.

Lochore Castle (also known as Inchgall Castle) is certainly a clue to this. Yet more recently, after the century long legacy of the coal pits had been cleared away and Nature was restored in the form of Lochore Meadows Country Park, it was getting harder and harder to see the old castle as trees and thick bushes sprouted around it and the fragile masonry crumbled away. That was when the archaeologists arrived. A collaboration involving The Living Lomonds Project, Benarty Heritage Group and Fife Coast and Countryside Trust enabled the outlines of the castle to re-emerge as the dead wood was pruned back and trenches were dug to give us a clearer view of what went on here in the past. And this is where our play begins …

Yes, we know some things about what happened here. But most of the things we know concern politics and wars, or the politicians and famous men who created them. We know the Romans passed through on their way to the camp at nearby Scotlandwell. We know that King David of Scotland gave the lands to a Frenchman, Hugh of Burgundy, to build his castle to protect the new Scottish kingdom. We know that Cromwell led his army through here, fighting a religious war. But what of the ordinary folk, who have lived and grown up and worked here for centuries? Do we know what it was like to be them? What of the generations of children who have played on the slopes of the old castle? Archaeologists, digging in the ground, can find clues. Things abandoned or buried that help us to put the pieces together of a time scattered jigsaw.

Our lead character, Jennie Lee, doesn't like school much, let alone history. She thinks it's not for her. Then she visits the Castle and goes on a wee journey and learns a few things. She even meets a teacher from long ago at

Glencraig School who has the same name as her. Neither of them know it - not yet anyway - but this teacher will go on to be a famous politician. One who makes a real difference. Not much of a difference if you are already a King or a General, a Captain or a Lord. But a huge thing if you are one of the folk who live in the shadow of the castle or the old Mary Pit. For Jennie Lee the teacher will go to help start *The University of the Air* or *The Open University* as we know it as now.

Who knows? One day, young Jennie might follow her. One day, you might too ...

The Real Jennie Lee...

Jennie Lee was born in Lochgelly on 3rd of November, 1904. Her Dad, James Lee, was a socialist and a member of the Independent Labour Party, an organisation that campaigned for equality and the rights of working people as well as to achieve home rule for Scotland. He influenced Jennie's political ideas. Jennie attended Beath High School. She was a gifted pupil and wanted to go to university but the family didn't have enough money. Due to a bursary awarded by the Carnegie Trust, who paid half her fees, Jennie was able to go to Edinburgh University. After graduating with a Master of Arts degree and a teaching qualification she returned to Fife. In 1929 she stood as the ILP candidate for North Lanarkshire in a by election and won the seat. She was the youngest MP at the age of 24 and one of only a handful of woman MP's in the House of Commons at that time. A fearless debater and campaigner for what she believed was right, her first speech was an attack on the budget proposals of Winston Churchill accusing him of "cant, corruption and incompetence". Jennie Lee married another politician, Aneurin Bevan, who helped to set up the National Health Service after World War Two. Jennie herself became Minister for Arts in Harold Wilson's Government in 1964. She was put in charge of creating the *University of Air* or The Open University which allowed working people who had missed the chance to study for a degree to go back and gain qualifications. They could study at home and learn from specially made tv programmes, sending essays and assessments to their tutor by post. Not an easy task when you are working and looking after a family. At the time, there were many people who opposed the founding of the Open University. Between 1965 - 67 Jennie Lee had to work and fight hard to make it happen. Since its founding The Open University has changed the lives of tens of thousands of people for the better.

In 1973 as she laid the foundation stone for the first OU library, she described the university as: *a great independent university which does not insult any man or any women whatever their background by offering them the second best, nothing but the best is good enough.*

Acknowledgement

I would like to thank all the staff and pupils at Benarty Primary School for their involvement, commitment and talent. Most of all for their warm welcome.

Special thanks are offered to Fiona Kerr and Kevin Sayer for ensuring Jennie Lee's Homework Project came to fruition.

William Hershaw

FIFE YOUTH ARTS

Manager:	Karen Taylor
Project Co-ordinator:	Andrew McDivitt

JENNIE LEE'S HOMEWORK PROJECT

Written by:	William Hershaw
Director:	Amanda Glover
Music:	Margaret Bennett
	Claire Saunders

BENARTY HERITAGE PRESERVATION GROUP

WORKERS' EDUCATIONAL ASSOCIATION (WEA)

Davie Reid

BENARTY PRIMARY SCHOOL – JENNIE LEE ARTS PROJECT

Drama:	Catherine Baker
Visual Art:	Hazel Terry
Digital Art:	Nik Balson
Filmmaking:	Graeme Rennie
Assistants:	Gillian Rennie, Catherine Higgins and Molly Herriot
Programme adviser:	Anne McBride

BOOK COVER ARTWORK

Saskia Brock, Dara Johnston, Alexander MacKenzie, Aimee Morrison and Abbie Paterson

First Performance of Jennie Lee's Homework Project
at the Lochgelly Centre
24th February, 2017
Characters/Cast

Jennie Lee:	Beth Adam
Dylan:	Brogan Williamson
Mum:	Kiaya McHale
Professor Delve:	Dan Kinnaird
Helen:	Katie Walkingshaw
Maggie Howker:	Bayleigh McKean
Ora:	Katie Bell
Centurion:	Ben Rafferty
Agrippa;	Dara Johnston
Balbus	Jennifer Anderson
Robert of Burgundy:	Evan Stritch-Burton
Jacques:	Kimi Anderson
Pilgrims:	Honey King, Shaunie McIntosh and Rhianna Notman
Tam:	Ali Hodge
Jockie:	Abigail Milligan
Guillaume:	Kaci Morrison
Willie:	Amber Coutts
Sir Walter Scott:	Aaron Hughes
William Adam:	Reece Izatt
Lizzie:	Summer Davis
Annie:	Aimee Morrison
Speaker:	Dionne Leslie
Teacher:	Paige McKenzie
Peggie:	Cooper Davidson
John:	Kimberly Dunn
Charlie:	Katie Martin
Alan:	Lucy Martin
Voice:	Kimberley Fotheringham
Soldiers/Miners:	Aimee-Lee Robertson, Megan Leishman Kyle Reid, Morgan Bryson, Paris Paton Lily Clemo and Codey Williamson

Jennie Lee's Homework Project

A play by William Hershaw

Act One, Scene 1

A living room. Jennie Lee is sitting up at the dining table not doing her homework. She is bored. Her big brother Dylan is sitting on the settee, engrossed in his computer game.

Jennie: Dylan?

Dylan ignores her.

Jennie: Dylan?

Dylan is pressing the controls furiously.

Jennie: Dylan?

Dylan: Shut up!

Jennie: Dylan, I'm bored, let's go out to play . . .

Dylan ignores her.

Jennie: Dylan, you've been playing that game for an hour. Let's go out and do something. We could play at football . . .

Dylan: Shoosh! I'm nearly at the next level . . .

Jennie: It's stopped raining Dylan . . .

Dylan: Wheest! You're interrupting my concentration, Jennie . . .

Pause.

Jennie: Dylan . . .

Dylan throws the controller down in exasperation.

Dylan: Now look what you did! I was nearly at level eight and
                     you spoiled it! That's the closest I've ever got. It's taken
                     me ages to get near it. Dylan, Dylan, Dylan! Why can't
                     you give me peace and do your homework?

Jennie: Sorry. But it's just a stupid game anyhow . . .

Dylan resumes his game.

Pause.

Jennie: Dylan?

Dylan: Aw naw! Whit?

Jennie:	Do you want to go to the park?
Dylan:	No.
Jennie:	Why not Dylan?
Dylan:	Why not? Because I don't want to . . .
Jennie:	Why not Dylan?
Dylan:	Why not? I'll tell you why not – because I don't want to be seen with my stupid little sister, that's why. Because I don't like going to the park. In fact, I don't even like going outside. Look out the window, see, it's raining. It's horrible and cold and windy. Yuk! Only an idiot would want to go out there on a wet Sunday. Why can't you leave me alone for just a minute and let me play my game? Do your history project like mum said.
Jennie:	I hate you! All you care about is your stupid computer games. You're not interested in anything else. It's not real, you know?
Dylan:	So? It's more interesting than playing with stupid wee lassies. Besides, it's educational. You learn stuff aboutwars and history. I got an 'A' pass for my project, remember?

Jennie:	(Puts on a silly voice and mimics Dylan) *I got an A pass for my project.* You're a swot and a geek. School's rubbish! I hate homework!

Dylan throws a cushion at Jennie. It misses and knocks over a vase of flowers.

Dylan:	See what you made me do now? I hate you!

Jennie:	I hate you back ten times over!

Enter Mum:

Mum:	What's going on? You've broken my best vase! Look at the mess – there's water spilled over the carpet.

Jennie:	It was Dylan. He threw a cushion.

Dylan.	It was Jennie. She moved her head away and let the cushion hit the vase . . .

Jennie:	Liar!

Dylan:	No, you're a liar!

Mum:	Quiet both of you! I'm sick of the pair of you fighting and bickering.

Dylan:	Mum, it was all Jennie's fault. I was sitting playing my game, minding my own business. I'm fed up with her!
Mum:	Jennie, have you finished your history project like I told you?
Jennie:	(Sullenly) No.
Mum:	You were supposed to do it on Friday night when you came home from school. But you didn't. Now it's Sunday afternoon and it still isn't finished. I don't want you getting into trouble at school. Go to your room and finish it.
Jennie:	That's not fair! I'm getting punished while Dylan gets off with it.
Mum:	Dylan did all his homework on Friday. Go to your room, young lady.
Jennie:	No, I won't! It's not fair!
Mum:	Jennie, for the last time . . .

Jennie storms out the living room. The front door is heard being slammed shut.

Mum: What am I going to do with that Jennie Lee? If it's not the neighbours complaining about her kicking a footballagainst their wall then it's the teacher saying she's not doing her work. Yet she's a kind hearted wee thing. I know as much . . . o dear, I hope she's not gone down to the Park. I found her the last time at Lochore Castle bothering the archaeologists at the dig . . .

Act 1, Scene 2

Backdrop of Lochore Castle. The two remaining archaeologists, Professor Delve and his assistant Maggie Howker are packing their tools away, pulling a tarpaulin over their trench. There is a tent with trestle tables with various finds on them. Jennie Lee runs on.

Professor: Hello there Jennie. You look like you're being chased by a wild bear. We're just packing things up for the night. You nearly missed us.

Jennie: Have you found anything old today?

Professor: Not much that's really old today, I'm afraid. Mainly mining stuff from the pit days. But still interesting. Maggie will show you what we've got if you go over to the table.

Maggie: Didn't think you were coming today Jennie?

Jennie: I had to stay in and do homework. Have you found anything new today?

Maggie: Not much. Let's see. Plenty old fishbones and fresh water mussel shells. You see, at one time the loch was much bigger. This castle was on an island and the water reached as far as the football pitch over there. The people who lived in the castle would row out in a little boat.

9

Jennie:	Have lots of people lived here?
Professor:	Oh aye – and lots have passed through here as well. That's what archaeology is Jennie. We're looking in the ground for evidence the people who lived here before have left behind. Mostly we're raking through their rubbish heaps and middens.
Jennie:	Why?
Professor:	Good question. So we can understand them and how they lived. If we can understand that much it may help us to understand ourselves and how we got here. We get to understand ourselves better through studying the past. We're the children of the people of the past.
Jennie:	I don't get it. But I like looking at this stuff from the olden days. And I love old stories.
Professor:	So you're interested in how your granny and granddad and their grannies and granddads lived?
Jennie:	I'm called after somebody famous from the past. I can't remember their name though. It was something to do with my great granddad, mum said.

Maggie:	Would it be Jennie by any chance? Listen, we won't be here much longer, Jennie. A few more days and then we'll have to fill up the trenches and put everything back as it was. Then we go back to the university to write up our report.
Jennie:	Oh!
Maggie:	You've been down almost every day. We'll miss you. Come and have a look at these things. Do you know what this could be?
Jennie:	No.
Maggie:	We think it's a piece of Roman pottery though we'll have to check. It was found on a farm a few miles from here and handed in. Just think: maybe a thirsty Roman soldier passing through on his way to the camp at Scotlandwell stopped for a rest and had a drink. And look at this – what do you think this can be?
Jennie:	It's like a bit of broken green glass.
Maggie:	It is – but it's green glass from the middle ages Jennie. When Robert of Burgundy, the first Laird of Lochore Castle came here and built his castle it must have been cold and damp and draughty. At some stage, either him or one of his ancestors put in small windows to block out the cold wind coming over the loch. We found an old shoe as well from the same period. And look at this . . . what do you think?

Jennie: It's like a medal. It has a picture of a lamb on it.

Maggie: You're right. It's called an 'Agnus Dei' medal. It means
                     the lamb of god. In the old days people would make long
                     journeys on foot to holy places in order to worship God.
                     They carried and collected medals like this – kind of like
                     to show where they'd been or where they were going.
                     Only   somebody lost or dropped this one, probably on
                     their way to the big cathedral at St Andrews.

Jennie: What's this rusty old thing?

Maggie: Compared to the other things it's not so old. It's called a
                     Davy Lamp after the inventor Sir Humphry Davy. Until
                     fifty years ago this whole area was where the coal mines
                     were. The miners used lamps like this underground.
                     They had a wick but the flame was enclosed in a mesh
                     screen which made these lamps safer to use when there
                     were flammable gases around. We found lots of coal
                     mining stuff: old boots, shovels, piece tins, clay pipes
                     the miners smoked. When they closed down the mines
                     they threw everything away. Sometimes we have to dig
                     through loads of it to get to the older finds. Anyhow,
                     that's us nearly done now. (Maggie begins to pack up
                     the finds and store them away.) Jennie picks up the
                     Davey lamp to look at it. As she does the stage lights go
                     down gradually. The stage grows dark. The Professor
                     and Maggie vanish into the shadows. The stage starts

to fill up with smoke. As the stage lights dim completely and Jennie is left in darkness, the Davey lamp lights up by itself casting a dim glow among the swirling smoke. The sound of a rushing wind grows louder and louder then stops suddenly.

Jennie: What's happening? Maggie! Professor! Where are you . . .?

Act 1, Scene 3

Lights come back up. The smoke begins to clear. Jennie stands on the stage alone and bewildered. Ora, a girl the same age as Jennie runs on stage. She is dressed in a deer and rabbit skin tunic. She grabs Jennie by the hand.

Ora: Quick now! We have to get out of the way!

Jennie: Eh? What's happening? Where am I?

Ora: Quick now! Over here – before they come!

Jennie: Before who comes?

Ora: The soldiers of course . . . follow me, we'll hide in the long reeds on the bank of the loch . . . follow me.

Ora drags Jennie over to the edge of the stage.

Ora: Get down! Keep your head down!

Jennie: I don't understand – who are you? Where's the Professor and Maggie?

Ora: I'm Ora. I lived in the Crannog.

Jennie: The what?

Ora: The house on the island in the loch. Now wheesht! I can
                        hear their footsteps.

Enter marching Roman soldiers from audience right, led by Centurion.

Centurion: Halt! We'll stop here for a rest. Only a few miles round
                        the hill and we'll be at the camp at Scotlandwell.

The soldiers relax, take off their packs and flop down on the ground.

Centurion: Careful now! Balbus and Agrippa – stand guard. We
                        have to be careful here. You can't trust these Picts. If
                        anything moves or comes near – throw a spear at it and
                        ask questions later. Got that?

Agrippa and Balbus: Yes Sir.

Centurion studies his maps.

Agrippa: Why always us?

Balbus: Aye, I could have being doing with a lie down on the
                        heather. My pack's killing me.

Agrippa: It's my feet. I've got blisters as big as eggs because my sandals don't fit.

Balbus: How far till we get to the fort?

Agrippa: He said it was around the hill. I hope they've got some decent supper there.

Balbus brings out a pottery jug.

Balbus: Don't let the Centurion see. I smuggled this in my pack. Here, have a swig.

Agrippa: Oh thanks! Just the job.

They drink thirstily. Balbus flings the empty jug into the reeds.

Jennie: Ouch!

Agrippa: What was that?

Balbus: It came from over there.

Agrippa and Balbus draw their swords and approach the reeds swishing and slicing.

Balbus:	Who goes there?
Agrippa:	Come out and surrender!
Centurion:	Right lads. Break over! Time to march. Into formation with you.

The other soldiers rise grumbling.

Centurion:	Agrippa, Balbus, what are you up to over there?
Balbus:	We heard a cry.
Centurion:	Probably just a bird – leave it. It's time we were out of here. Join the ranks.
Agrippa:	Ok, Sir.

The soldiers begin to march off left. Agrippa and Balbus fall in. Swirling smoke fills the stage. Ora and Jennie look up.

Ora:	Phew! That was close. I thought they were going to find us.
Jennie:	I still don't understand . . . where am I? Who did you say you were?

Ora: I'm Ora. Don't worry Jennie. I know it's confusing. I'll
                look after you. That's why I'm here.

Jennie: I need to get home. My Mum will be worried. Maybe see
                you later, Ora. Thanks.

Jennie gets up and walks toward centre stage.

Ora: No, Jennie, Come back! There's more soldiers coming. I
                can hear them marching. Quickly, over here! They'll be
                here in a minute.

Jennie hesitates for a second. Noises are heard off stage left. Jennie scurries
back to Ora and crouches down.

Jennie: What now?

Ora: Watch.

Enter Robert of Burgundy, a Norman knight with his soldiers and retainers
from the left. He holds up his hand to command them to stop.

Robert: *Arrêtez l'hommes! C'est ici l'endroit.* David, the King of
                Scots must have been kidding when he gave me these
                lands and said it was a paradise. Look at it! It's raining
                and cold. What can you grow out here? And where are
                the servants he promised?

Jacque:	Sire, maybe it'll work out ok. The locals will have gone into hiding. They'll be a lazy crew, like peasants everywhere. But we'll soon put them to work and let them know who the new boss is around here.
Robert:	We'll have to take care though. We must find a strong safe place to build our castle. A stronghold where these barbarians can't ambush us and murder us in our beds.
Jacque:	There's an island out there on the loch that looks good. It seems it was built on before because I can see ruined stones and wood. We can use these to make a start. Then we'll make the locals quarry stone, cut down trees and fetch it out there. There'll be plenty fish in the loch for us to eat as well.
Robert:	Good thinking Jacque. Right – let's get started. We'll head over to the high ground on the South side and make our camp for the night. Tomorrow we'll make a start. (Sighs) Sometimes I wish I had never left my father's warm gardens and vinyards in France. And all to become the master of this unwelcoming land. Now Robert of Burgundy has become Robert of Lochore. *Nous allons nous déplacer, pauvre paresseux.*

Robert and his men exit to the right.

Jennie:	They looked different.

Ora: What?

Jennie: They were different from the other soldiers.

Ora: It's always a different lot. Different yet the same.

Jennie: What do you mean?

Ora: They go back and forward all the time, back and
                forward. Their clothes change, that's all. The main thing
                is that we have to keep safe – out of sight. Soldiers are
                bad news. Hush! Who's that coming now? I don't
                recognise the footsteps.

Enter from the right the Pilgrim with rosary beads, hooded and praying. The
Pilgrim halts and looks over the loch. Then goes over beside the bank and
scoops up some water to drink.

Pilgrim: Holy Father, I thank you for the gift of this water to a
                weary pilgrim.

Ora: Shoosh!

Pilgrim: And who is this here, hiding in the reeds? Two song
                birds maybe? Step forward children, for you have
                nothing to fear from me.

Ora and Jennie step forward hesitantly.

Pilgrim: Why are you hiding?

Ora: We were hiding from the soldiers.

Pilgrim: Ah – always the same story. The little ones are the
                victims. Don't be frightened of me. I won't hurt you. I'm
                just a poor pilgrim on my way to Saint Andrews.

Ora: A pilgrim? What's that?

Jennie: Oh, I think I know that one . . .

Pilgrim: I'm making a journey, children. It's been a long trip. I'm
                headed to the place where the bones of Andrew the
                apostle of Jesus and the patron saint of Scotland
                are kept at in a kirk in a place called Kinriemont.

Ora: Andrew? Why, I've never heard of him.

Jennie: Why would you want to visit some old bones?

Pilgrim: Ah – that is a good question, child? It is hard to explain.
                One time I was lost and unhappy. I prayed to Andrew
                to speak to God on my behalf. I suppose I thought
                God himself would be too busy to listen. My prayer was
                listened to, and things got better for me. So I suppose

I'm making this trip as a kind of "thank you." But looking in the eyes of you two, I think you both may be lost and far away from home as well. I want you to take this. It's a medal we pilgrims carry around with us for protection. It's got a picture of a little lamb on it. You'll have to share it between you and I hope it helps to bring you home. Now bless you both. I must go now before night falls. Goodbye and good luck.

The Pilgrim exits to the left.

Jennie: Wow!

Ora: You keep the medal, Jennie.

Jennie: Really, Ora, are you sure? Thanks.

Swirling smoke fills the stage. Marching is heard from the left.

Jennie: More soldiers.

Enter from the left a ragged army of men in plaids and kilts. Their weapons are bill hooks, swords and sticks. The men march on. One lags behind and stops. His pal comes back for him.

Tam: Haw Jockie, are you all right there?

Jockie: Aye, fine Tam. I've a stone in my shoe, that's all.

Tam: A stone in your shoe? – Who do you think you are? You're lucky to have shoes for your feet. Most of the lads haven't. Mind you, look at the state of them. They're falling to bits, man. Neither wonder you're falling behind. It's a wonder you don't trip up and fall on your face.

Jockie: Naw, they're a braw pair. Tanned deer hide. Passed down from my auld Grandfaither.

Tam: Aye, they look it as well. Man, they're minging! Acht, you'll never make a sodger, Jockie. Get yourself sorted and join the lads. It's a long way to Stirling and William Wallace needs every man he can muster to see off the English.

Jockie: Aye fine, I'm coming. I just hope it's worth ruining braw shoes for.

Tam: Worth it? You know it's worth it, Jockie. Even if we both don't come back from Stirling Bridge, it'll be worth it if we win our freedom from Edward's tyranny. We have a chance here to build a nation.

Jockie: Is that what this William Wallace says?

Tam: We have no choice, man. Do you want your children and grand children to grow up as slaves?

Jockie: Of course not. But I'm thinking, what difference is it
            going to make if I get shot by English arrows? At the end
            of the day, it'll still be the lairds and the lords who are
            running the country. Like him over there in the loch in
            his big fancy castle, drinking fine wine from France in
            his painted chamber with its wolf skin rugs and green
            glass. It'll make no difference to me and mine. I'll still
            have to be getting up early to work in his fields and my
            daughters will still have to bow and kneel and skivvy
            and serve him and his French speaking family.

Tam: The Wallace says it won't be like that. Here's our chance
            to try something that's never been done. A nation of folk,
            from the richest to the poorest, lairds, burgers,
            peasants, bonded together by what they share in
            common. Besides, if you have to be ordered about
            by some stuck up laird, wouldn't you prefer it to be a
            Scottish Laird at least?

Jockie: Aye, whatever . . .

Tam: So get that stone out of your shoe and let's catch up.
            C'mon! We don't want to miss the fight.

Jockie: Aye, aye, I'm coming, haud yer wheesht! I'm only here
            because your Peggy said someone needs to look after
            you . . . and the fact that I love a guid stushie.

Jockie reluctantly removes his shoes and throws them away. They nearly hit
Ora and Jennie.

Tam and Jockie exit to the right.

Jennie: This is the busiest place I've been to. It's like trying to
                 cross a motorway. Is it always like this, Ora?

Ora: Oh aye. You've got to be careful.

Jennie: So where do you stay, Ora?

Ora: Close by. My family were the first to live here. We've
                 always been around.

Jennie: That's funny, I've never seen you. You don't go to
                 Benarty or Saint Kenneth's?

Ora: People are coming. Duck down.

Enter two well dressed gentlemen, Sir Walter Scott and William Adam from
the right.

Scott: Mind your feet there, My Lord! This ground is so clarty it
                 reminds me of the fields around my home in the Borders
                 when the Tweed floods.

Adam: You do your home an injustice, Sir. Abbotsford is a fine
                 building – my grandfather would have been proud to
                 have built it. But enough of this calling me Lord – that's

fine for formality and servants but we are equals, Sir Walter. William's fine.

Scott:

You have so many titles, William. One does not know where to begin. Lord Lieutenant of Kinross-shire. Lord Chief Commissioner of the Jury Court. Solicitor General for Scotland. Where do I stop?

Adam:

Yet you who choose to be anonymous have lasting fame through your books that I will never attain. (They both laugh. Sir Walter produces an eye glass and surveys the landscape.)

Scott:

Boggy it may be, but good Captain Park was to be praised for trying to drain the loch. It was not his fault that it fills up again whenever it rains. And it does – plenty and often!

Adam:

They say that for three seasons of the year it is too wet to yield a profit. A pity. Look yonder at the castle ruins. Why it has almost returned to being an island again.

Scott:

Yet you have continued the good work upby at Kelty that your Grandfather and father started.

Adam:

The trees are well rooted and thriving. Most of the land has been enclosed. But the greatest benison is the treasure hoard, the black crop that lies under the land. My engineers tell me that Blairadam is built on coal. It stretches for miles under our feet and is the

most Northern deposit in Britain. So mining has begun.
We have started tunnelling. It was my grandfather's
belief that everything should be pleasing to the eye
and seemly but also have a use. The Blairadam estate
exemplifies this: the trees grow and are pleasing to look
on, meanwhile they hide the diggings and the spoil
heaps made by the workers below the ground. A perfect
arrangement.

Scott: And how do your workers feel?

Adam: They are born to manual labour. Whether in a field or
              beneath the ground, what difference to them?
              They are well provided for. I have built good clean
              houses for them which they can keep for life,
              provided that they remain industrious and
              temperate and godly.

Scott: What was that? I saw something move through my eye
              glass. In the reeds over there! Is it two deer – have a look
              yourself, William.

Adam: Ah – it is two children. Youngsters but old enough to be
              usefully employed. Maybe they are waifs who have run
              away from their masters. Come here children! Come
              over here and account for yourselves.

Ora and Jennie leap up and run off stage left. The stage begins to swirl with
smoke. Scott and Adam stand transfixed. Lights go down.

Act 2, Scene 1

Lights go up on stage.

A platoon of volunteers dressed in World War 1 uniforms march on briskly from the left. They are polished and immaculate. They are all in good humour and are singing and smiling as they swing their arms.

Soldiers:

> Every road through life is a long, long road,
> Filled with joys and sorrows too,
> As you journey on how your heart will yearn
> For the things most dear to you.
> With wealth and love 'tis so,
> But onward we must go.
>
> ***CHORUS:***
> *Keep right on to the end of the road,*
> *Keep right on to the end,*
> *Though the way be long, let your heart be strong,*
> *Keep right on round the bend.*
> *Though you're tired and weary still journey on,*
> *Till you come to your happy abode,*
> *Where all the love you've been dreaming of*
> *Will be there at the end of the road.*
>
> With a big stout heart to a long steep hill,
> We may get there with a smile,
> With a good kind thought and an end in view,

We may cut short many a mile.
So let courage every day
Be your guiding star alway.

CHORUS:

Keep right on to the end of the road,
Keep right on to the end,
Though the way be long, let your heart be strong,
Keep right on round the bend.
Though you're tired and weary still journey on,
Till you come to your happy abode,
Where all the love you've been dreaming of
Will be there at the end of the road.

The soldiers exit to the right.

Offstage heavy gunfire is heard. Shells scream and explode. Machine gun and rifle fire is heard along with muffled cries. Lights flicker on and off. Gradually the sound of warfare subsides. Music is heard off stage. A lone piper plays the tune "The Battle of The Somme". Enter the platoon from the right, led by the piper. They are greatly changed. Half of them are gone and the survivors limp across the stage slowly and wearily as if in a daze. Their uniforms are muddy and ripped. Some are bandaged, some are on crutches. One soldier leads a man who is blinded. They do not sing. They exit stage left.

Enter Jennie and Ora from the left:

Jennie: Can we rest here, Ora? I'm tired. I think we've been
                     going round in circles. I thought I heard noises a
                     minute ago. Like shooting and bagpipes. This is a weird
                     place. I wish I was back home! Oh, I'm going to be in big
                     trouble with Mum. Oh dear! Will I ever get back home
                     again? I think I'm stuck here forever with you, Ora.

Ora: Don't worry, Jennie. We'll get you home somehow. Now listen, you must do exactly as I say . . .

Jennie: I miss mum. Even Dylan.

Ora: Don't fash yourself, Jennie. Now, there are people coming through here again . . .I can hear them coming.

Jennie: O no! Do we have to hide again?

Ora: No, I don't think so. I have a good feeling about this . . . and somehow they are connected with you. They may help you to get home.

Jennie: How?

Ora: I don't really know how. But trust me . . .

Jennie: Aye? Ok then . . . I think. What do I have to do?

Ora: When the next lot come through all you have to do is run out and join them. Follow them where ever they go . . . and you'll be fine, I think.

Jennie: And what about you Ora? Are you not coming with me?

Ora: I'm afraid I can't, Jennie. I have to stay here for now.
                But don't worry. I'll be fine.

Jennie: Ocht Ora . . . don't leave me now. We could be pals.

Ora: We are pals already. Here, take this for luck, it's a
                necklace made from antler bones. It'll keep you safe.

Jennie: Why, thank you Ora.

Music and singing is heard offstage.

Ora: That's them. Run when I say and join them, Jennie.

Offstage is heard:

          The people's flag is deepest red,
          It shrouded oft our martyred dead,
          And ere their limbs grew stiff and cold,
          Their hearts' blood dyed its ev'ry fold.
          Then raise the scarlet standard high.
          Within its shade we'll live and die,
          Though cowards flinch and traitors sneer,
          We'll keep the red flag flying here.

Enter the striking miners. Preceded by a makeshift brass band. They carry a
banner saying "Not a minute on the day, Not a penny off the pay." Wives and
children follow them.

Ora: Now Jennie, join them!

Jennie: But what about you?

Ora: Just go, Jennie, I'll be fine.

Reluctantly Jennie runs forward, turning to look back. Ora has slipped away off stage already .

Two of the mining children approach Jennie.

Lizzie: Who are you?

Jennie: I'm Jennie.

Lizzie: I'm Lizzie and this is Annie. You don't come from round here, do you Jennie?

Jennie: Erm . . . not really.

Annie: Don't worry, we'll look after you.

While the children are talking the grown ups are preparing for the speech. A soap box is dragged on for the Union official to stand on. The miners and their wives sit down to listen. The children are at the back.

Jennie:	What's happening?
Lizzie:	They're going to make speeches.
Annie:	It's a bit boring really but it's better than being in school.
Lizzie:	Our teacher said that because it was a special occasion we could come along and listen for a bit. Why are you not in school, Jennie?
Annie:	Hush! He's starting. . .
Speaker:	Comrades, welcome . . . we all know why we're here today. We all know what's led up to this so I won't go into details. There are men here today who fought in the Great War. Most of us have friends and relatives who died in that war. We have all made sacrifices. Our leaders told us that when the war was over we would live in a land fit for heroes. Now our Government is telling us that the country is crippled with a huge debt because of that war and that we are the ones who will have to pay it back. Is that right, do you think?
All:	No!
Speaker:	Now they want us to work in the mines – already a dangerous and exhausting job – they want us to work for longer and for less pay. Do you think that is right?

All:	No!
Speaker:	Now they are saying that the coal mines don't pay their way. It is too expensive to run them and they can bring in cheaper coal from abroad. Because of this we have to accept their conditions. Is that right?
All:	No!
Speaker:	Then we have no choice. We only have one thing we can do. And that is to withdraw our labour, to go on strike so that the mines will close and they will make no more profits from our hard work until they agree to treat us better. Is that right!
All:	Aye!
Speaker:	Comrades, I will not lie to you. It will be a hard struggle and there is no guarantee that we will win. Our families will be hungry, there will be no money. They will turn us out of our homes if we cannot pay the rent. They will imprison us when we protest. Do you still think it is worth it?
All:	Aye!
Speaker:	Then let us march now to the gates of the pit. Let us go now and make them understand we will never give in!

Loud cheers: The band starts up. The children dance and skip in excitement. The march heads off stage to the right. The children follow on at the end and Jennie goes with them.

Teacher: Right children! Back to school now! Form a line.

The children grumble.

Children: Aw Miss! Do we have to? Can we not join the march!

Teacher: No, I'm afraid that's not possible. Listening to the
                            speeches is one thing. It's important for you all
                            to hear what is going on in the community around you.
                            But going on the demonstration is too dangerous. I don't
                            want any of you getting hurt. Now – back to class quickly!

The children move off reluctantly. Jennie hangs behind.

Lizzie: Quick Jennie! Join our class.

Jennie joins the class and they file off to the left.

Act 2, Scene 2

The school playground. Boys are playing football. Girls gather together.

Lizzie: Where's your big brother, Albert, Peggie?

Peggie: He left school on Friday. He was fourteen. He's away down the Mary Pit today.

Annie: Lizzie fancies him.

Lizzie: No, I dinnae! I was just asking – anyway, I'd rather go out with Bert than that long drip Stanley that you fancy. (to Jennie) He's the mine manager's son you know and he goes to school in Dundee. You want to see Annie when he comes home in the holidays. She hangs about the big house just for a keek at him.

Annie: No, I don't Lizzie and you know it. I only go there to take my big sister her pieces. She's their maid.

Peggie: Hmph! You wouldn't catch me being a maid. I'd rather die than go into service. That's what my mum says.

Annie: Your mum used to work at the pitheid picking out stones from the coal belt. My mum told me.

Lizzie:	So what?
Jennie:	My mum says that I've to stick in at the school so that I can go to university.
Girls:	Eh?
Jennie:	What's wrong?
Peggie:	Don't you know girls don't go to university, Jennie? Certainly no miners' lassies like us. How could we ever afford it?
Annie:	My dad says a women's job is to cook, clean and look after the bairns.
Lizzie:	Hey, that was good of Miss to give us an extended playtime after letting us go to hear the speeches.
Peggie:	Aye, I suppose so. But she'll ring the bell and call us in soon.
Jennie:	Miss must have gone to university to become a teacher?
Annie:	Aye, but she's no like us. She doesnae speak like us.

Lizzie:	Mind you, wouldn't it be braw to grow up and do whatever you wanted, to go where ever you wanted . . . maybe one day it will be like that. . .
Annie:	You sound like thon union fellow on his soapbox. "One day we'll all be equal and we'll hae strawberry jam on our pieces!"
Peggie:	Hey, Jennie, would you like to join our band?
Jennie:	Eh sure, what band?
Peggie:	We're forming a band to go round the streets to earn pennies for the soup kitchen. Hiya boys, over here now for band practice . . .

The boys stop their football and come rushing over.

Peggie:	John's the only one with a real instrument. He plays the cornet in the brass band.

John takes a battered cornet from a case and proudly blows a few notes.

Peggie:	Dan plays the moothie. . .

The children form a makeshift band including comb and paper, tambourine, a ukele missing a string, a stone jar for bass.

Peggie: Right everyone. On the count of four. One, two, three, four . . .

A loud and enthusiastic racket starts up. The children sing.

A gang o chaps, including me, had naething else tae do,
We thocht upon a caper tae raise a bob or two,
So we held a general meeting in a close ye understand,
And came tae the conclusion that we wad start a band.

CHORUS

I'll gang roon wi the hat my boys,
I'll gang roon wi the hat,
I'll tak care o the chink, chink, chink, I'm awfou guid at that,
I'll gang roon wi the bouncey bounce, as lively as a cat,
I'll be the heid cashier o the band, so I'll gang roon wi the hat.

We made oor first appearance in a quiet lookin street,
But we had tae keep oor eyes upon the bobbies on the beat,
We sang a dizzen sangs an mair, surrounded by a crowd o weans,
But though we did oor level best got sweet naethin for oor pains.

CHORUS

I'll gang roon wi the hat my boys,
I'll gang roon wi the hat,
I'll tak care o the chink, chink, chink, I'm awfou guid at that,
I'll gang roon wi the bouncey bounce, as lively as a cat,
I'll be the heid cashier o the band, so I'll gang roon wi the hat.

This band turned oot the worst, and we couldna mak a cent,
Although we made an awfou noise everywhere we went,
The haill o us were hungry, and fou o discontent,
So I proposed that every chap should pawn his instrument.

39

CHORUS

I'll gang roon wi the hat my boys,
I'll gang roon wi the hat,
I'll tak care o the chink, chink, chink, I'm awfou guid at that,
I'll gang roon wi the bouncey bounce, as lively as a cat,
I'll be the heid cashier o the band, so I'll gang roon wi the hat.

Enter teacher from the left ringing a handbell furiously. It takes a while for the children to hear her and stop playing and singing.

Teacher: My goodness, what a racket! I'm already in trouble with the Headmaster for taking you to the march. Do you want me to get sacked? Now put those things away and get into line while I take the register.

The children form a line. The teacher calls out their names individually then ticks her register. As each name is called, the pupil walks smartly into the classroom.

Teacher: John Brown?

John: Present, Miss.

Teacher: Go into class. Mind take your cornet, John. Charlie Campbell?

Charlie: Present, Miss. In you go, but leave that football with me Charlie.

Teacher:	Lizzie MacDonald?
Lizzie:	Present, Miss.
Teacher:	Annie McCormick?
Annie:	Present, Miss.
Teacher:	Alan Paton?
Alan:	Present, Miss
Teacher:	Peggie Munro?
Peggie:	Present, Miss.
Teacher:	My goodness! We've got one left over! Who are you, child?
Jennie:	My name's Jennie, Miss.
Teacher:	But where have you came from?
Jennie:	I met Annie and Lizzie at the march and they said it would be ok to come along with them. But if it's a problem I'll just go away.

Teacher:	Did they indeed? Well, I'll be having a wee word with those two. But no, you can't just go. I'm assuming that you've just moved into the area?
Jennie:	Aye, something like that . . .
Teacher:	Well, really Jennie, your Mum or your Dad will have to come down to the school and get you enrolled at the office. What did you say your full name is?
Jennie:	It's Jennie Lee, Miss.

Teacher stops writing in her registration book.

Teacher:	What did you say?
Jennie:	My name's Jennie Lee. I'm named after somebody famous but I can't remember who it is . . .

Teacher laughs.

Teacher:	There's no one famous with that name that I know of, Jennie – not yet anyway – but here's a coincidence. We two have the same name. I'm called Jennie Lee as well.
Jennie:	Wow! Really, Miss?

Teacher:	Yes. We may be related even. Though I suppose it's a common enough old name. Listen Jennie, here's what I want you to do. Take this note along the corridor to the school office. It's beside the Headmaster's room. Give Mrs. Meickle, the secretary, the note and then she'll take your details and enroll you temporarily till a grown up is able to come along to the school. It's a dark old corridor but don't be frightened. The lights are not working so take this old Davey lamp with you – some of the children are scared to go along there. They say there's a ghost but you're a sensible girl and don't believe rubbish like that, do you? Then when you've finished come back and join us in class. Now, have you got all that?
Jennie:	Yes, Miss.

Teacher exits to left. Jennie is left on her own with Davey lamp. Stage grows dark.

Jennie:	Well, I suppose, I can either run away again or keep going along this dark corridor. What a choice! Ora's gone and there's nowhere else for me to go to. Here goes.

Jennie continues along a very dark corridor. At the far end there are two doors. From underneath one door a bright light spills.

Jennie:	This is creepy, I don't like this much!

Jennie reaches the door and after some hesitation knocks timidly. There is no answer. She knocks again more loudly. A voice from inside says "Come in!" Jennie hesitates then opens the door. The stage is flooded in brilliant white light.

Act 2, Scene 3.

Backdrop of Lochore Castle. Jennie is sitting on the ground beside the overturned trestle table, dazed and rubbing her head. Around her, looking concerned, are Mum and Dylan, Professor Delve and his assistant Maggie Howker.

Jennie: Ouch! What happened?

Mum: It's ok darling, you're fine. You got a knock on the head.

Dylan: Are you ok Jennie? I'm sorry for being horrible to you?

Jennie: Mum – Dylan's being nice. Is he ok?

Mum: He's just concerned. That's all. He came out to look for
            you when you ran out the door. He ran back for me
            when he saw that you'd knocked yourself out.

Jennie: Thanks Dylan.

Dylan: It's ok?

Jennie: So what happened?

Professor:	Let me see. How many fingers am I holding up Jennie?
Jennie:	Three.
Professor:	That's good. But you'll have a fine bruise on your forehead for a while. I think you'll be fine, Jennie but you're best to go to A & E to get it checked out. Just to be on the safe side. We'll give you and your Mum a lift.
Jennie:	Yes, but what happened?
Maggie:	You bent down to pick something up Jennie. I don't know what. Just then there was a gust of wind that seemed to come from nowhere. It blew the Davey lamp off the table and it hit you on the head and stunned you . . .
Jennie:	Oh right . . . that explains it all . . . so it was all a dream then?
Maggie:	What was a dream?
Jennie:	Oh nothing.
Professor:	It was some gust of wind! It blew the tarpaulin and all our finds away. We'll have to look for them tomorrow. The main thing is that you are all right.

A light appears left of stage. Ora appears. She waves to Jennie. Jennie waves back.

Dylan: Who are you waving to Jennie?

Jennie: Can't you see?

Mum: It's time we got this young lady to hospital to get checked out.

Maggie: Yes.

Ora points to her neck. At first Jennie does not understand. Then she digs into her pocket. She produces Ora's necklace. Quickly she thrusts it back.

Jennie: Professor?

Professor: Yes, Jennie?

Jennie: The finds you lost – the glass, the pottery, the shoe, the 'Agnus Dei' medal?

Professor: Yes?

Jennie: Don't worry. I know where to find them.

Professor: Sure, Jennie. We'll look tomorrow . . . now you get in the car and tell me if you start to feel sick.

Jennie: Sure, Professor. Professor?

Professor: Yes, Jennie?

Jennie: I've decided I want to be an archaeologist when I leave school. What qualifications do I need?

Professor: That's great news. We'll talk about it in the car. Jump in!

They walk off stage right. A car engine is heard starting. The car drives off. Ora takes centre stage.

Ora: The roe deer's in the rowans,
                The sloe black burn is never still,
                A hawk hings high and hovers,
                The geese are gaun ower the hill,

                As the gloaming faas aa things are lown,
                The early star catches fire.
                A houlet is smoolin ben the mirk,
                Speirin for mice in the byre.

                Ilka hour, ilka day,
                The roads are aye thrang,
                Wi fowk dauding aboot
                Tae whaurever they gang.

There's ayeweys a pilgrim,
At aa times o the year,
Comin fae yonder,
Gingin til there.

Some gangrels tramp doulsome,
Some gleg sauls tred herty,
Some come fae the muin
Or the back o Benarty.

I am Time's witness,
I've see them aa,
Restless as the burn
As it tummel's and faas.

For I was the firstlin
Born in the thaw,
When bear and wild wolf
Prowled in the snaw.

And I'll bide here aye
Through winds kind and ill,
Till the ice freezes up
As heich as yon hill.

The End.

Resources

- *I'll Gang Round Wi The Hat* by Robert MacLeod. 'Robert MacLeod: Cowdenbeath Miner Poet', introduced and edited by Margaret Bennett. Published by Grace Note Publications, 2015.

- *Keep Right On To The End Of The Road* by Harry Lauder

- *The Red Flag* by Jim Connel (.1889)